The Wonder of
MANATEES

To Edward Murphey Coffield (a fellow manatee lover and part-time muse) and all kids who love manatees.

— Patricia Corrigan

For a free color catalog describing Gareth Stevens Publishing's list of high-quality books and multimedia programs, call 1-800-542-2595 (USA) or 1-800-461-9120 (Canada). Gareth Stevens Publishing's Fax: (414) 332-3567.

Library of Congress Cataloging-in-Publication Data

Bauman, Amy.
    The wonder of manatees / by Amy Bauman and Patricia Corrigan; illustrated by John F. McGee.
        p. cm. — (Animal wonders)
    Includes index.
    Summary: Text and photographs introduce these gentle brownish gray mammals that live in the water.
    ISBN 0-8368-2663-9 (lib. bdg.)
    1. Manatees—Juvenile literature. [1. Manatees.] I. Corrigan, Patricia, 1948- . II. McGee, John F., ill. III. Title. IV. Series.
QL737.S63B38   2000
595.55—dc21   00-039516

First published in North America in 2000 by
Gareth Stevens Publishing
A World Almanac Education Group Company
330 West Olive Street, Suite 100
Milwaukee, WI 53212 USA

This edition is based on the book *Manatees for Kids* © 1996 by Patricia Corrigan with illustrations by John F. McGee, first published in the United States in 1996 by NorthWord Press, Inc., Minocqua, Wisconsin, and published as *Manatee Magic for Kids* in a library edition by Gareth Stevens, Inc., in 1996. Additional end matter © 2000 by Gareth Stevens, Inc.

Photographs © 1996: Doug Perrine/Innerspace Visions, Cover, 28-29; Daniel J. Cox/Natural Exposures, 6, 18-19, 36-37, 42; Jeff Foott, 7, 10, 15, 16, 30-31; Art Wolfe, 12; Brandon Cole, 23, 24, 34, 41, 46.

Printed in the United States of America

1 2 3 4 5 6 7 8 9 04 03 02 01 00

The Wonder of
MANATEES

by Amy Bauman and Patricia Corrigan
Illustrations by John F. McGee

Gareth Stevens Publishing
A WORLD ALMANAC EDUCATION GROUP COMPANY

The story of mermaids began long ago. Sailors at the time said they saw mermaids — beautiful sea creatures that were half-woman, half-fish — and heard them singing. Today, we know the story of mermaids is a legend. How did it begin?

Many people believe that what the sailors saw were manatees. Manatees are bulky, gray mammals.

They have two short flippers and broad, flat tails.

Manatees live in water, but they do not look anything like the mermaids described by the sailors! Manatees do not have long hair or fishlike tails, and they don't sing. Instead, manatees have chubby faces, squinty eyes, and stubby whiskers. They are often called "sea cows."

Manatees are slow-moving and gentle animals.

They grow to be about 10 feet
(3 meters) long and can weigh
a ton — or even more!

There are three species, or types, of manatees: African manatees, Amazon manatees, and West Indian manatees. Some manatees live in waters around Florida. Although they are called Florida manatees, they are actually West Indian manatees.

Manatees eat sea grasses and
plants found at the bottom of
rivers and along sea coasts.

They hold the plants with their flippers. Manatees have three fingernails on each of their flippers.

Manatees come to the
surface of the water every
few minutes to breathe air.

Under the water, manatees make sounds. They talk to each other with chirps, whistles, and squeaks.

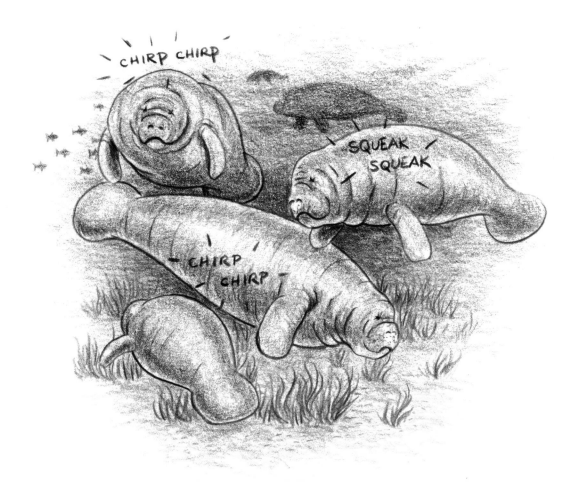

Manatees spend their days eating, resting, and swimming. They also like to snuggle, hug, rub noses, and play with each other. At times, manatees even play a game that seems like "Follow the Leader!"

Manatees swim slowly, twisting and turning in the water. Even though they are slow, they can travel long distances.

Manatees have been on Earth a long time. From fossils, scientists can tell that ancient relatives of manatees lived about 35 million years ago.

The manatee also has a relative that is alive today — the dugong. Dugongs live in the Pacific and Indian oceans. They are about half the size of manatees.

Dugongs have smooth bodies and long, flat, forked tails. Guess what? They are sometimes called "mermaids!"

In the 1700s, scientist G.W. Steller studied another manatee relative that was discovered in the Bering Sea. Much bigger than manatees, Steller's sea cows were 30 feet (9 m) long and weighed several tons.

Hunters killed these sea cows for their meat and hides. By 1768, Steller's sea cows became extinct.

Sadly,
the Florida
manatee is
in trouble
today. It is
an endangered
species.
Less than
two thousand
of these
manatees
are still alive.

Why are there so few manatees? Many die when they are injured by boats. Others die from water pollution or from eating plastic litter. People who build near shorelines can also destroy manatees' food and homes.

To protect manatees, Florida now has speed limits for boats in areas where manatees live. In many countries, it is against the law to kill manatees. Time will tell if this magnificent creature will be able to survive.

Female manatees give birth just once every two to five years. Usually, one baby is born at a time. Baby manatees are called calves. They are about 4 feet (1.2 m) long and can weigh 65 pounds (29 kilograms) at birth. A calf drinks its mother's milk, which comes from under her flipper.

A mother and calf stay together for about two years. Mothers teach their calves to find food, places to rest, and the best travel routes.

People enjoy watching manatees in wildlife parks and other habitats. Many people know manatees are in danger, and want to help save the animals.

When people report seeing an injured or sick manatee, wildlife workers come to the rescue. Rescuers take the manatee to a special animal hospital. They treat wounds, remove fishing lines from around a manatee's fin or tail, or take care of orphaned calves.

Wildlife rescuers do all they can to make sure manatees are healthy and safe.

Animals are happiest in their natural habitats. That is why the rescuers return manatees to the wild as soon as their injuries have healed.

Wildlife workers often become friendly with the gentle manatees. Manatees might swim up close to their human friends. They might even take tasty treats right from a worker's hand!

Today, many people realize just how special manatees are — even if they are not exactly like the mermaids in legends!

Glossary

calves – the young of certain mammals such as cows, whales, and manatees

endangered species – certain animals that have become rare and are close to becoming extinct

extinct – no longer alive

flippers – the broad, flat limbs that help a manatee swim and eat

habitats – the places where animals or plants live in nature

legend – a story passed down through time that may or may not be true

mammals – animals with hair or fur that feed their young with mother's milk

orphaned – without a mother or father

sea cow – a name often used for some water mammals, such as manatees and dugongs

Index